Dear Rhea...

.. a little bit of london for wherever you find yourself next.

Love you.

Ada

xxx

Published by Influx Press

Office 3A, Mill Co Project. Unit 3, Gaunson House, Markfield Road

London. N15 4QQ

www.influxpress.com

First published 2014

Printed and bound in the UK by the Short Run Press Ltd, Exeter

ISBN 978-0-9927655-5-2

Outside Looking On

Chimène Suleyman

Influx Press, London

For

Emetullah Şehitoğlu and Süleyman Oğuz

Contents

Introduction

It would be all too easy to call it a reclamation. This megatron sitting apart from the skyline. This part of London they promised to us when they were creating it. My father, a man who cannot pass a building site without offering acute improvements on the development of it, littered our house with building magazines. In the late 80s it was as though Canary Wharf, or 1 Canada Square, was growing from these front pages in our living room. We would live there one day. Work there. We would eat and socialise. This better life that immigrants, and non, are promised at some point in return. It was for us, they said. It is, of course, no one's. Perhaps not even those who work within it, as interchangeable as the market it supports. Disconnected from the rest of the city it seemed lonely.

We were all lonely once. A rather unexceptional emotion. Aren't we all lost and missing? It is not this that interests and never has. Because, when you knew to look, it was everywhere. From a house in Finchley, at the tip of a market in Clapton.

From a dentist's office in Muswell Hill, a bedroom in Deptford, a hospital in Archway, a train in Essex, a bus in New Cross.

From my living room in neighbouring area Westferry, a power cut took the houses until there was only the humming of silence that we are not used to. Slightly beyond us Canary Wharf, raised on a dark platform, remained lit. A lighthouse, a compass, solar system. I could go on. It was a companion, if nothing else. You will find the memory of past friends and lovers anywhere. You will be reminded of memoriesand jokes in a littered crisp packet when the recollection is strong enough. In short: Imagine anything, anywhere.

Chimène Suleyman - London, 2014

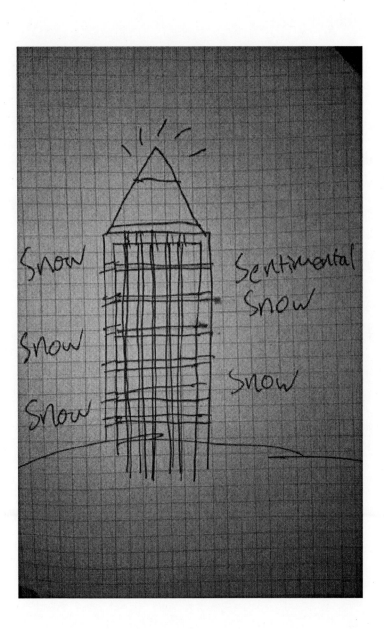

Wearing Hooves

We spoke openly of not loving the other.
To be more precise: we spoke of those
we loved instead. He described her hair,
black, he impressed fingers upon it,

her speech a powerhouse mimicked by
well-oiled recollections. Him,
almost handsome, crumpled. Misplaced
behind hands too vast for their weight.

Turning my face to the screen
the image sang somewhere behind us.
I shall tell you about those lovers
who saw twice, their hearts go up in flames.

Tears, a draped blanket covered time and,
Let me become the shadow of your shadow,
the shadow of your hand,
the shadow of your dog. He wept.

The windows beyond windows, they watched us
and beneath them, away from it all, "Just listen" he said.

The Passenger

She has two girls, who each night she will meet at the
end of road. Pretty girls who will watch candlewax

drip from table at Pizza Express, whose job it will be
at 2am to scrape with butter knife and their nails.

"I am sorry for my friends," he points at suits and
reaches for her breast. She will eat her meal perched

at kitchen freezer, quick mouthfuls of gravy, wipes
down balsamic from sides, all this to pay for ASOS tomorrow.

"Don't mind them," he will say. With each Jägerbomb
they put a shotglass to ear and listen for the sea.

Her mother meets them each night at the end of their
road. Streetlights disguised behind heavy-duty stilts.

She will meet them when it is late like this
to take them back.

When She Calls

The crane outside the window licks its lips
pokes fun at clouds, swings big dig
but only telephone wires are visible, you say:
its nervous system stretched. You are

a good liar, I think.
There is a crane outside the window,
licking the air with its hook, blocking
my view.

Take the Time, Heron

to understand why we are here. I have
shown you the marina, now on our left, with the water we mustn't touch.
Beside us, the perfect outlines of a glowstick town, an unmissable
constellation of argon. But I must ask you, Heron, to not eat the yogurt pot
you have found on the side of the road. The round edges of the plastic
will push through your drainpipe-neck until it is scratching, tapping
at your intestines and taking apart your ventricle.

I am showing these boats to you, Heron; imagining the coastlines
drawn in childish vertical blue pencil. Here we will sail
the world. And it is usually as the peaks of daylight arrive
that the lights in office windows are switched off, and
so the sky is emptied of stars. Do not let me eat
the yogurt pot, Heron. I have tried it before.

It Might Have Been the A140

I say I hate the countryside
because it is designed badly.
I keep saying it until it winds you up.

A bee flies through the window
as we are driving and stings me
on the arse, which feels apt.

Pulling over, you suck the sting
and laugh. We must laugh. You say,
Well, there's no going back from this.

I know you are right. As I keep lying
about hating the countryside.

Tartan

A new home will not become as such until the fridge is
full for its first time.
With this, in heavy bags of shopping,
her fingers remembered him.

Brian, the Theorist

He says his bones were killing him, these twisting carnivals
beneath beechwood skin, it was from the pleasure found in the
top quarter of beer in which his voice was guided, accented
in Happy Mondays or Hungerford Arms. He would tell it to her
straight; this acquaintance, arm-skin slumping like a handbag
from pits. She talked inquisitively, an investigator, from
his neck a garland hospital-badge where he portered down
the road and fasttrack appointments came like extra chips
from your fournightsaweek local. Don't worry yourself, he says,
this face of an oak leaf; cancer and all that damn shit. It's better
to sweat in the night. It gets you up in the fucking morning.

Coffee Table

It says 07/03/06 on the table.
For Hot Euro Boy Action Call . . .
A friend's number carved into it.
Small holes, burns from rollies
dropped from ashtrays when sleep
took over. When 'Rainy Day
Woman' played the radio.

I turn the radio up to fill room
and put daffodils over the holes.

Balcony (part one)

From the balcony he had attempted
to throw him. A walkman between
mattresses embedded between stains.
Soon they would tear it to the ground,
these windows like dry ponds, a spacebar
uninterrupted. Even where doors were
newspapers, it heard farewell.

A Man Not Forestalled

for Blake

We danced from our seats, the tables full
between us and the next drink. When I
think about it, he put my hair between
his fingers that night, my back against floor,
and sighed. It was the night I kicked a man
but, you must understand, I asked first;
the night he urged – the smile we know
so well – I steal the mug, floral print,
from a boiler-room cab station.
The wine was broken. And under unsparing
skyline, your father and I, we danced
for you. I held his hand, or perhaps
he held mine. And it is from our seats
we are watching the weather change.

George

I pour whiskey down my
my throat like I
am filling
a vase. And put
cigarettes like stems inside.

Brian, the Historian

Everyone here says they knew the Krays.
Over twenty years; all he hears – the Krays.

He raises an arm, *Mike!* No one knew the Krays:
he waves. They were fucking gangsters.

The Worried Well Worrier

I am certain it is cancer. I can feel it
collecting in my vagina like retribution,
a fork scratching against a plate.
It is this sound that grinds
between my brain. "I can't have children,"
I tell him. Though this is based on the death
sentence I have submitted to my womb
written in celebrity demise, guided by guilt.
A plane has crashed, the month is March
yet recession will not end, so. I can feel;
it is a tumour. I am certain of this.
As certain as I am the key stopped catching,
predictable like the light atop that spells
medical notes in Morse-code; for isn't this a sign?
Each leaflet turned to corner, the general

practitioner's surface in baby-vomit cover,
this beep and tap of a phone screen by half
clawed nails. It is unlucky
to find the missing sock. The bulk
of timber warped, how could we ever use it now?
I will not repeat-call the doctor
when my science is this broken horse saddle
we spoke of. Each counted strand
on the hairbrush, it is malignant.
It must be? Genitals disowning me, for aren't
the pages of this book frayed. I am certain –
whatever it is – that it is my fault. Isn't this
what we tell our daughters?

I go to stay in the empty house
and water the plants every day.

They die anyway. Things break
and he comes round daily

like a maintenance man
to fix things. I think

he thinks he's fixing me.
And I let him because we need it.

We stay drunk for months
so neither of us will recognise

when nothing needs fixing
anymore, other than us.

£6.99 House White

There's a breed of them round these ends,
praying to Arsenal, thugs for arms.
Smokes a spliff by the bus
and says thanks for coming home.

Tramshed or Any Other Place
(a love poem)

It is possible when I threw meat at that waitress
we started our best memories: Six wrinkles
held symmetrically in place by giggles.
The smell of an ice bucket.

Held in reversed photos
of thumbs-up and pulling faces;
I showed your image to a car salesman
who slipped it inside the sunshield.

We are box sets of Sopranos episodes
willing sick-days to last longer.
Great sandwiches we have bragged about
created from everything in our fridge.

And all I can think about are your exes.
Clicking onto Facebook, swiping
through the photos, thinking:
Really? Her? How the fuck?

Mevlevi

With the side of a shoe he kicked, and then bit
the top of a Calippo. The child missed
in that way children do. Distracted by the ice-cream
van swimming laps. Melody weaved corners,
this familiar ditty that marked schoolruns
to much later. Straightened in the doorway

breasts loose in coral tunic, her veil reaching
into brickwork, these flattened shoulders
commanded the streets. Skillet-burnt hands
tipped to tarmac and heaven. Spinning
on left foot, her skirt a bird low to the ground,
as ice-cream vans changed their song for her.

Ping

The black and white cat is fat.

The black and white cat is fat with depression.

Feed him. Watch him lie between

steps of a ladder and bask in the sun.

Do not look up at the view.

You will only lose your appetite.

Instead of Working

I rearrange my books until they look right. Then I take them down and put them back up based on feeling. They don't feel right because it is the only place my obsessive compulsive plays out. And when I find all the books you gave me I read the notes you wrote me inside them and forget about the stories. I take them all down again and put them back up based on looks. The ones with notes in look best together.

Postcard

Can you see it? I left it here for you.

Bendigo

The sniffer dog shrugs his shoulders. He's been
working the station three years and can
tell you about the FTSE – symptom of the job.

He knows the ones who drop coins in the charity
bucket (tourists) and there's no such thing
as a local. He got the job through a popular

agency, its listing of successful clientele:
guide Labradors, rescue dogs, cadaver tracking,
homeless helpers, the sled dogs and herding.

The days are slow but at least he gets to stretch
his legs and enjoy the air. It would be nice
to be stroked once in a while.

Brian, the Government Official

If he wasn't a porter, he'd be prime minister.

He'd middle the wages, like communism,

somewhere central and everyone gets a taste.

Then he'd raise the wages of porters so he could

quit politics and work that again. He shouldn't

complain. Some people don't have jobs.

Brian, the Relationship Counsellor

He has never been in love. Name him
a man who has. Or woman, for that matter.
But he's watched a woman pee from behind
an open door. After, he's seen television shows
with her next to him. Fallen asleep, chin
an ungainly position on his chest. Thinking
about it, he has probably been in love.

Cultivating

And when you offered that pained expression
through a bus window, I suppose
you would have already known
that you were done; something you would later
blame me for although you had already decided
she would be your life,
the messages, the language lessons.

You were kind to say the foxes reminded you
of me, but what you really meant was they walked
lost when others were asleep. And when the fox
gave birth in my garden, I watched them, like rats, suckle;
she beneath shade of damp leaves, blinking
at daytime, unafraid to be in sight. Well done,
I thought; you've come a long way.

Balcony (part two)

The pale board went five high floors short of the estate.
Its bricks less so than the copper piping, so close,
a stare as though to say
So close, look, *we were so close.*
Your van left the street and with it I waited by window to wave.
You hadn't turned,
not this time.
You curved right.
Where eventually the boarded site comes down,
hidden in breeze blocks.
The *No parking* sign is an empty car park. Nowhere
to hide, the fire brigade pulled in first.

Dragging bailiffs, road cordoned, so they shouted, turn around,
turn around Madame, they said, go back.
I live there, *turn around*, and I hadn't wanted to.

Sunday

They are speaking about sofas. He is right, the brown leather
                    looks great against the wall. Someone
is refilling wine, red, from a height that indicates only great
                    confidence and it is all pay-rise chit-chat a tea-
set with leaf pattern, dodgerblue, across rim left by someone's
                    grandmother. The cream sauce is heated,
thank god. Across the table a baby cries. The impetigo raises
                    daytime sooner. Not to worry.
The braised artichoke has been seasoned. These houses, with
                    refitted bathrooms. Where is best for a second home?
It is steep to frame a painting. And all I am wondering about is
                    the order of Nirvana lyrics in my head.

Smollensky's

I am wearing the patterned leggings purposefully
to irritate the straight-cuts and tulips. Expensive
in my hand, the wine, no tastier than the ice cubes
drowning inside. *Well done for following your dreams,*
is something they like to say. But his boss made his way

up from an estate, and don't you forget it. Everyone
is given a *heads up* out there, *taking it offline, drilling* and
backfilling like the dentist who lives below me. He catches
the tattoos on my arms, their ottoman shapes. And in his best
phone-answering voice he saved this one for last;
Islam, sell it to me.

Inland

for Nikesh

The black lentils found us first.

They broke through windows to tell us they were here.

Stomachs bulging at belts so we would know.

Dear Boss from 'Smollensky's'

I could smell my grandmother on Morris Street. A familiar
smell of heat, and sweat, and molohiya, which itself smells of
heat and sweat. And in the car garage under the arches her
smell walked with me. When the strange man tried to grab
my legs on seeing the shorts I had braved for the first time this
season, I heard her voice, saw my father, a child, run, and my
grandfather follow, *why have you stopped?* I imagine he would
have asked. So my grandmother tells him, tells us all really,
for it was she who was the storyteller, that she would rather
stand still than be made to walk behind any man. And her
smell accompanies me home, until I stir it into my tea with
the wooden spoon she left me. It was her land they were busy
fighting for, and no one noticed the old thinning headscarves
in her cupboard, cared for, or wanted, and I drank the tea,
remembering them neatly folded in my wardrobe upstairs.

To Each, a Memorial of Sorts

Would I come to the funeral, the back of a shoe
sinking in soft ground. Would we hug, limbless
sleeves knitted into the other. Would we
shake hands, fingers, naked in grasp.

I could nod. Grieved lips that spoke, or
should I care for how I looked? Of course not.
But should my hair be raised, whiter,
neck free, you must know it is only coincidence

you preferred it this way. Would we laugh
as night progressed. Hushed between
memories only we shared. That I am left
with only the untimely death of an imagined other.

The only place I may envision holding you again.
Between carvings on the edge of stone; thy will be done.

Pancakes in Bartlett Park (Balcony part three)

She pulled flour from her satchell.
Fuck you. She pulled flour from her satchell.
And he, pointing at pyramid, prayed forgiveness.
Looming beneath, 3,960 lights, they
applauded, fuck you. Rubbing eggs,
hair, assault clouded by flour. Fuck you.
White rain. Sprayed against it *Capitalism*
is for Cunts. 3,960 would always know.
Fuck you, she said, leaning from window,
I watch, tighten her veil, I watch, drink
in hand, we watch, flour and eggs in hers.
On his knees, all it had taken was flour and eggs.
Let me explain;
there was little more I could do
but smile, eggs and flour. Above,
middle finger to the sky. She said it
in flour and eggs; be the woman that you want.
Raise a glass. Pull the window shut.

The Danse Macabre

As if they know: The end.

On a street outside. He raises her. Just above head.

Turn radio volume high. Car door open.

Dance together. Twirls: once, twice, once again.

There is nothing left to see.

Yesterday, But Not How The Beatles Told It

I've imagined it perfectly; the moment I tell you
I'm married.
I'm married,
I will say. And you will land on your knees
like old films dictate, cutting them on something sharp
on the way down. It does not matter what. You will forget
to eat, consuming only balls of mozzarella, hovering over sink,
biting into them like wet apples.
Smoking my favourite cigarettes
you will lie with your head on the table, stomach pushed
into the corner, discarding the insurance deals/ water bills/
out-of-date voucher.
The same song plays on repeat as you have stayed like this for
years, trying to make sense of it all.

Or you will smile and simply say, *That's nice, congratulations.*

Customer Service Survey

And when the email arrived I wondered
why you had bothered: *Saw this, and
thought of you*. As if an unkind nudge
to order takeaway, or receipt for online cab.

Perhaps what I am trying to say is
I expected *more*. Not of you, but
the email. A picture in it's attachment
of when we ate lunch by the canal,

an MP3 of our favourite jokes. Would
there be a video link to those fucking
awful cakes I baked? No bother.
Instead this: a suggestion for a book

I rather hated. How could this

have taken years to write, I wondered.

I considered replying. Of sending a recipe

for a dish, or song you might like in return.

There was nothing left to say. Yet I read it again to be

sure.

Beloved,

I cannot remember how you take
your tea. It is better for us both this way.

The Altercation

was never truly about the Oyster card.
That the machine had summoned noise as though
to rattle coins in pocket, incorrectly. It was not,
entirely, because of his tone. An office-chair
turning into creaks, churlish, the hair on his nose.
Confined by dark jeans and lapels upturned.

When had moccasins become trend again?
The feud was not – as he had said – because
of my attitude. Behind us inaudible bellows
of *E'enen Saander*. From the train I thought
of your deaths. On a platform above Millwall
stadium were minarets where you imagined them.

To Whom This May Concern,

I waited patiently by Westferry Circus. I doubt you would recognise the bench as only rain fell to the seat beside. The boat turned, a light winked once behind; how pleased you must be for such a grand lighthouse – a compass simply for you. To whom this may concern,

I thought you should know I kept fingers warm by smoking, that we have since worn jeans too tight, mouths covered in wine; we had long forgotten how to dance. I listened only to the echo of your footsteps, yet in this time we have eaten summer puddings, and given birth, for it is not only the old who die. I have hooked oysters under tongue, pulling in such

a way to show the lines that make us older now. It is time, tick, remember time, and I have gone off boiled eggs, but I am straying from the point, which is; I didn't know it could snow without you. I thought I should say that it is arguable – and no doubt incorrect – that the sky is clearer here, for sleepless birds are as frazzled as the rest of us. To whom this may concern,

I am not angry with you – whoever you are – the bench was meant for me, you see, it is a must to keep an empty chair if we are truly to stay sane. You want to leave, don't you? Who can blame you, if not me. And when the sun was on its way the lights in windows were switched off, so the sky was emptied of stars. I must tell you, forever was mistimed, make no mistake.

For when I see it I don't know if I think of you, but when you see it, please – whatever you do – don't forget me.

Acknowledgements

Endless thank you goes to Influx; Gary Budden and, in particular, Kit Caless for the opportunity to complete this collection and showing it sense when there was none. There will unquestionably be opportunity even here for Kit to make better.

Those who have sent, and continue to send, Canary Wharf photos have humoured this obsession to entertaining limits.

Thanks is always due to Niven Govinden, Stuart Evers, Gavin James Bower, Suzanne Azzopardi, and Katherine Solomon for your encouragement and friendship throughout the years.

A special thank you is owed to Nikesh Shukla who has been not only a friend, but a mentor and brother. To Musa Okwonga, Rosie Knight, Joshua Idehen, Tim Wells and Sabrina Mahfouz who never fail to find the best direction, and point to it.

Thank you to Michael Horn and Jessica Fagin for not allowing quitting to become a thing. Arron Smith, who endured hundreds of poetry nights when this all began, for which I am both grateful and sorry. Aaron "Sir" Murphy, you made the process of writing not a chore but a conversation a glass of whiskey sits well beside.

Thank you to Chay Carter who has bore the brunt of this yet still produces beyond human levels of support and love, even when I am not deserving.

The largest thank you must go to my parents, from whom the support is so great there are not enough words to say "thank you" with.

Chimène Suleyman was born in London. *Outside Looking On* is her debut poetry collection. She also writes on gender and race for online and mainstream publications such as the *Independent*. She represented the UK for poetry at the International Biennale, 2011.

photo (c) Meghna Gupta

INFLUX
PRESS

Influx Press is an independent publisher specialising in writing about place.

We publish challenging, controversial and alternative work written in order to dissect and analyse our immediate surroundings, to blur genres and to produce site-specific fiction, poetry and creative non-fiction.

www.influxpress.com